EMMANU...

Winning Her Heart Back: A Man's Guide to Rekindling Love

Contents

1

Chapter 1: Understanding the Journey of Love

Love is a profound and complex emotion, a journey that often takes unexpected twists and turns. To win her heart back, you must first understand the nature of this journey, for it is a path that both of you walk together. Love is not a static destination but a dynamic process, and comprehending its various stages is the foundation upon which you can rebuild and rekindle your relationship.

The Phases of Love

Love evolves over time, passing through different phases. It often begins with the exhilarating experience of infatuation, where everything about your partner seems perfect. You might remember the butterflies in your stomach and the constant anticipation of seeing her.

However, this honeymoon phase eventually gives way to reality. In the second phase, you'll discover imperfections and differences, leading to occasional conflicts and disagreements. This can be a challenging period, as the initial intensity of the relationship wanes, and you must learn to navigate these differences.

The third phase is the mature, enduring love that follows. It's a love that has weathered storms, overcome challenges, and grown stronger. It's the love that lasts a lifetime if nurtured and cherished.

The Cycles of Love

In addition to the phases, love operates in cycles. It's not a linear progression but a series of ebbs and flows. There are moments of intense connection and moments of distance. Recognizing these cycles can help you navigate the changing tides of your relationship.

The Importance of Self-Reflection

Understanding love also involves self-reflection. Take a moment to contemplate your role in the relationship. What have you contributed to its ups and downs? It's essential to be honest with yourself and acknowledge your shortcomings. Self-awareness is the first step toward personal growth and positive change.

Communication and Empathy

Successful navigation of the journey of love hinges on effective communication and empathy. Listening and understanding your partner's feelings, needs, and desires are vital. Open, honest, and non-judgmental conversations can bridge the gaps that often form between two people in a relationship.

Conclusion

In this opening chapter, we've delved into the complexities of the journey of love. Love is not static; it's a dynamic process that involves phases and cycles. It requires self-reflection, communication, and empathy to thrive. Now that you have a foundational understanding of the nature of love, you're better equipped to embark on the path to winning her heart back.

In the following chapters, we'll explore strategies and practical advice to navigate the phases and cycles of love, rebuild trust, and reignite the passion that brought you together in the first place. By the end of this journey, you'll not only have won her heart back but also enriched and strengthened your connection in ways you may have never thought possible.

2

Chapter 3: The Art of Effective Communication

Communication is the cornerstone of any successful relationship. In this chapter, we explore the vital role that effective communication plays in winning her heart back and rebuilding a strong, loving connection.

Listening with Empathy

Effective communication begins with active listening. When your partner speaks, practice empathetic listening. This means not just hearing her words but also understanding her emotions and perspective. Here's how to master empathetic listening:

1. Be Present:
   - Give your partner your full attention when she's talking. Put away distractions, make eye contact, and show that you genuinely care about what she's saying.

2. Reflect and Validate:

- Repeat back what she's said to ensure you understand correctly, and validate her feelings. Phrases like "I hear you" or "I understand how you feel" can be powerful in showing empathy.

3. Avoid Interrupting:
   - Let her express herself without interruptions. This demonstrates respect for her voice and her thoughts.

Open and Honest Communication

To rekindle love, you must be open and honest in your communication. This means sharing your thoughts, feelings, and concerns with transparency. Here are some tips for fostering open and honest conversations:

1. Choose the Right Time and Place:
   - Find a suitable setting for important discussions where both of you can focus without distractions.

2. Use "I" Statements:
   - Frame your thoughts and feelings using "I" statements, such as "I feel" or "I think." This approach is less accusatory and more about sharing your perspective.

3. Avoid Blame and Criticism:
   - Refrain from blaming or criticizing your partner during conversations. Instead, focus on expressing your needs and desires.

Conflict Resolution

Conflicts are a natural part of any relationship, but how you handle them is critical. This chapter delves into conflict resolution strategies, including:

1. Active Problem Solving:

- Work together to find practical solutions to your issues, aiming for compromise and understanding.

2. Avoiding Escalation:
   - Be mindful not to escalate conflicts by using hurtful words or actions. Keep the conversation constructive.

3. Taking Breaks:
   - If a discussion becomes too heated, it's okay to take a break and revisit it later when both of you are calmer.

The Power of Affectionate Communication

Love is not just expressed through words but also through actions. Show affectionate communication through gestures, compliments, and small surprises. Let her know that you cherish her and the relationship.

Conclusion

Chapter 3 emphasizes the significance of effective communication in rekindling love. By listening with empathy, being open and honest, resolving conflicts constructively, and expressing affection, you set the stage for rebuilding trust and nurturing a deeper emotional connection. In the chapters to come, we'll continue to explore techniques and strategies for revitalizing your relationship, with effective communication as the bedrock of your efforts.

3

Chapter 2: Reflecting on Your Relationship

efore you can rekindle the flames of love, you must take a step back and reflect on your relationship. This chapter delves into the importance of introspection, understanding the past, and evaluating the present to build a stronger foundation for the future.

The Power of Reflection

Reflection is a powerful tool for self-awareness and personal growth. When it comes to your relationship, taking the time to reflect on both your individual and collective experiences is crucial. Consider these key aspects of reflection:

1. Acknowledging Past Mistakes:
   - Reflect on past actions and decisions, both positive and negative. Understand how they have shaped your relationship.

2. Identifying Patterns:
   - Recognize recurring patterns in your interactions and conflicts. Are there habits or behaviors that have been detrimental to your relationship?

3. Gratitude and Appreciation:
   - Reflect on the positive aspects of your relationship, the moments of joy, and the things you appreciate about your partner. Gratitude can help shift your perspective.

The Role of Communication

Effective reflection also involves open communication. It's essential to create a safe space where you and your partner can discuss your thoughts and feelings honestly. Here are some communication tips for this phase:

1. Active Listening:
   - Practice active listening when your partner shares their perspective. This helps build empathy and understanding.

2. Non-Judgmental Approach:
   - Avoid making judgments or assigning blame during these conversations. The goal is to gain insight, not to point fingers.

3. Mutual Reflection:
   - Encourage your partner to engage in this reflective process as well. Their insights can be valuable in understanding your relationship dynamics.

Taking Responsibility

Part of reflecting on your relationship involves taking responsibility for your actions. This means admitting when you've made mistakes and showing a genuine willingness to improve. Taking ownership of your part in any conflicts or issues can be a powerful step towards rebuilding trust.

Setting Goals

As you reflect on your relationship, consider setting goals for the future.

What would you like to achieve together? What kind of relationship do you want to build? Having a shared vision can help guide your efforts to rekindle the love between you.

Conclusion

Chapter 2 is all about pausing to reflect on your relationship. By acknowledging the past, identifying patterns, expressing gratitude, and fostering open communication, you lay the groundwork for the journey ahead. In the following chapters, we'll explore strategies to address specific challenges and work towards rebuilding trust, reigniting passion, and nurturing a lasting, loving connection. Your willingness to reflect and take positive action is the first step in winning her heart back.

4

Chapter 4: Rebuilding Trust and Intimacy

Trust and intimacy are the cornerstones of a healthy and loving relationship. In this chapter, we will explore the essential steps to rebuild trust and rekindle the intimacy that may have faded over time.

The Importance of Trust

Trust is the foundation upon which love is built. It's the belief that you can rely on your partner, that she will be there for you, and that you can share your deepest thoughts and feelings without fear. To rebuild trust, consider the following:

1. Honesty and Transparency:
   - Be open and honest about your thoughts and actions. Transparency is essential to rebuilding trust.

2. Consistency:
   - Consistency in your words and actions is vital. Make sure your actions align with your promises.

3. Patience:

- Rebuilding trust takes time. Be patient and understanding of your partner's need to heal.

Nurturing Emotional Intimacy

Intimacy is not solely about physical closeness. Emotional intimacy is equally crucial. It involves a deep connection, understanding, and shared vulnerability. Here's how to nurture emotional intimacy:

1. Deep Conversations:

- Engage in meaningful conversations that delve into your thoughts, dreams, and feelings. Share your inner world with your partner.

2. Express Vulnerability:

- Allow yourself to be vulnerable with your partner. Sharing your fears and insecurities can strengthen the emotional bond.

3. Show Affection:

- Physical touch, hugs, kisses, and affectionate gestures are essential to building emotional intimacy.

Rekindling Physical Intimacy

Physical intimacy plays a vital role in rekindling love. It's not just about sex but also about physical closeness, affection, and desire. To rebuild physical intimacy:

1. Set the Mood:

- Create an atmosphere conducive to romance and intimacy. Plan date nights, use scents and lighting to set the mood, and be present in the moment.

2. Communicate Your Desires:

- Openly discuss your desires and listen to your partner's needs. This communication can lead to a more fulfilling physical relationship.

3. Explore Together:
   - Experiment and explore together. Trying new experiences and maintaining a sense of adventure can reignite the spark in your physical relationship.

Forgiveness and Healing

If trust has been broken in your relationship, forgiveness and healing are essential. Both you and your partner need to be willing to work through past issues and let go of any grudges. This is a process that may require professional help or counseling.

Conclusion

Chapter 4 focuses on the critical elements of trust and intimacy. Rebuilding trust requires honesty, consistency, and patience. Nurturing emotional and physical intimacy involves deep conversations, vulnerability, and affection. By embracing these principles, you are on the path to restoring the core elements of your relationship and rekindling the love that first brought you together. In the following chapters, we will explore additional strategies to strengthen your bond and build a lasting, loving future.

5

Chapter 5: Nurturing Emotional Connection

Emotional connection is the heartbeat of a loving relationship. In this chapter, we explore the importance of fostering emotional intimacy, understanding your partner's needs, and nurturing a deep, lasting connection.

Embracing Emotional Vulnerability

Emotional connection thrives when both partners allow themselves to be emotionally vulnerable. It's about sharing your innermost thoughts, fears, and dreams. Here's how to embrace emotional vulnerability:

1. Create a Safe Space:
   - Make sure your partner feels safe to express herself without judgment. Encourage open and honest conversations.

2. Active Listening:
   - Actively listen to your partner when she shares her feelings. Offer support and understanding rather than solutions or advice, unless asked for.

3. Share Your Emotions:
   - Be willing to share your own emotions and experiences. This reciprocity deepens the emotional connection.

Empathy and Understanding

Understanding your partner's perspective and feelings is key to nurturing emotional connection. Empathy helps you bridge the gap and show that you truly care. Here's how to cultivate empathy:

1. Walk in Her Shoes:
   - Try to see situations from her point of view. Understanding her feelings and reactions is a powerful form of empathy.

2. Validate Her Emotions:
   - Acknowledge her feelings and experiences. Even if you don't completely understand, validate her emotions.

3. Be Patient:
   - Emotional connection often takes time to develop and strengthen. Be patient and let it evolve naturally.

Quality Time Together

Spending quality time together is essential for building emotional connection. It's not just about being physically present but about truly engaging with each other. Consider these suggestions:

1. Date Nights:
   - Plan regular date nights to create special moments and experiences together.

2. Unplug and Disconnect:

- Put away devices and focus on each other. Being fully present in the moment strengthens emotional connection.

3. Shared Hobbies and Interests:
  - Find activities or interests you both enjoy and pursue them together.

Gratitude and Appreciation

Expressing gratitude and appreciation is a simple yet powerful way to nurture emotional connection. Acknowledging what you love and value about your partner reinforces your emotional bond.

1. Compliments and Affection:
  - Offer compliments and affectionate gestures to let your partner know she is loved and cherished.

2. Gratitude Journaling:
  - Keep a gratitude journal together, where you both write down things you appreciate about each other.

Conclusion

Chapter 5 delves into the importance of nurturing emotional connection, embracing emotional vulnerability, practicing empathy, spending quality time together, and expressing gratitude and appreciation. These elements are the building blocks of a deep, lasting emotional bond. By dedicating time and effort to nurturing this connection, you can continue on your journey to winning her heart back and strengthening the love you share. In the upcoming chapters, we will explore strategies to reignite passion and overcome relationship challenges, building a more profound connection.

6

Chapter 6: Rediscovering Romance and Passion

Love thrives on passion and romance. In this chapter, we explore the art of reigniting the flames of desire and infusing your relationship with the excitement of romance.

The Role of Romance

Romance is more than just flowers and candlelit dinners; it's about creating moments that make your partner feel cherished and loved. Consider these tips for rediscovering romance:

1. Thoughtful Gestures:
   - Small, thoughtful gestures like leaving love notes, planning surprise dates, or simply cooking her favorite meal can go a long way.

2. Spontaneity:
   - Inject spontaneity into your relationship. Surprise her with unexpected adventures or acts of love.

3. Keep Dating:
   - Continue dating each other, even if you've been together for a long time. These special outings can rekindle the romantic spark.

Passion and Desire

Passion is a vital component of any intimate relationship. It's about desire, anticipation, and connection. Here's how to reignite passion:

1. Open Communication:
   - Discuss your desires and fantasies with your partner. Sharing these intimate thoughts can lead to a deeper emotional and physical connection.

2. Physical Affection:
   - Physical touch, kissing, cuddling, and holding hands are essential for maintaining physical intimacy.

3. Variety and Exploration:
   - Be open to trying new things in the bedroom. Exploring together can rekindle passion and desire.

Maintaining Connection

As time passes in a relationship, it's easy to get caught up in daily routines and responsibilities. However, maintaining a strong emotional and physical connection requires effort. Here's how to keep the connection alive:

1. Time for Each Other:
   - Dedicate time to each other regularly, even when life gets busy. This reinforces your connection.

2. Connection Rituals:
   - Develop rituals or routines that are special to your relationship. These

could be a shared morning coffee or a bedtime routine.

3. Regular Check-Ins:
   - Schedule periodic check-ins to discuss how you're feeling about your relationship and what you can do to strengthen it.

Embracing Adventure

Injecting adventure into your relationship can reignite passion and excitement. This might involve taking spontaneous trips, trying new activities together, or embarking on personal growth journeys as a couple.

Conclusion

Chapter 6 emphasizes the importance of rediscovering romance and passion in your relationship. Romance is about creating moments of love and connection, while passion is about desire and connection. By embracing both, you can reignite the flames of your love and create a relationship filled with excitement and anticipation. In the upcoming chapters, we will continue to explore strategies for overcoming relationship challenges and building a lasting, loving future.

7

Chapter 7: Overcoming Relationship Challenges

Every relationship faces its share of challenges, and how you navigate them can significantly impact your connection. In this chapter, we'll explore the common challenges couples encounter and strategies to overcome them.

Common Relationship Challenges

1. Communication Breakdown: Misunderstandings, conflicts, and a lack of effective communication can lead to a breakdown in your relationship.

2. Trust Issues: Trust can be eroded due to past mistakes or external factors. Rebuilding trust takes time and effort.

3. Conflict and Resentment: Unresolved conflicts and long-standing resentment can create a barrier between partners.

4. Changing Priorities: As life evolves, individual priorities and goals can shift, affecting the dynamics of your relationship.

5. External Stressors: External factors like work stress, financial pressures, or family issues can put a strain on the relationship.

Strategies for Overcoming Challenges

1. Effective Communication:
   - To address communication breakdowns, focus on improving your communication skills. Practice active listening and express your thoughts and feelings openly. Seek to understand your partner's perspective.

2. Rebuilding Trust:
   - Rebuilding trust requires consistency, transparency, and patience. Keep your promises and demonstrate through actions that you can be relied upon.

3. Conflict Resolution:
   - When conflicts arise, approach them with a problem-solving mindset. Avoid blaming and criticizing each other. Instead, work together to find mutually acceptable solutions.

4. Addressing Resentment:
   - If resentment lingers, engage in open conversations to uncover the source of these feelings. Forgiveness and a commitment to moving forward are key.

5. Aligning Priorities:
   - Address shifting priorities by discussing your individual goals and values. Finding common ground and supporting each other's ambitions can strengthen your connection.

6. Managing External Stressors:
   - When external stressors affect your relationship, work as a team to manage them. This may involve setting boundaries, seeking support, or finding ways to de-stress together.

Seeking Professional Help

In some cases, overcoming relationship challenges may require the assistance of a therapist or counselor. Professional guidance can provide a safe and structured environment for addressing complex issues.

Conclusion

Chapter 7 focuses on recognizing and overcoming the common challenges that relationships face. By practicing effective communication, rebuilding trust, addressing conflicts and resentment, aligning your priorities, and managing external stressors, you can navigate these hurdles together. The key to rekindling love is not the absence of challenges but how you face and conquer them as a united couple. In the chapters ahead, we will continue to explore strategies for sustaining and growing your connection.

8

Chapter 8: Being a Supportive Partner

Support is the cornerstone of a strong and loving relationship. In this chapter, we'll delve into the various ways you can be a supportive partner, fostering an environment of trust, empathy, and encouragement.

Understanding Support

Support is not limited to financial assistance or problem-solving. It encompasses emotional, psychological, and practical elements. Being a supportive partner means you are there for your loved one through the highs and lows of life.

Emotional Support

1. Active Listening: Be attentive when your partner needs to talk. Show empathy and understanding without rushing to provide solutions.

2. Validation: Acknowledge your partner's feelings, even if you don't fully understand them. Validating her emotions shows that you care.

3. Empathy: Try to see the world through your partner's eyes. Empathizing with her experiences creates a deeper emotional bond.

Practical Support

1. Sharing Responsibilities: In a relationship, sharing household and financial responsibilities demonstrates partnership and support.

2. Taking Care of Each Other: When one of you is unwell or going through a tough time, taking care of each other is a powerful display of support.

3. Solving Problems Together: Approach challenges as a team. When you face difficulties, working together to find solutions is a form of support.

Encouragement and Growth

1. Cheerleader Role: Encourage your partner in pursuing her dreams and goals. Celebrate her successes and provide motivation during setbacks.

2. Personal Growth: Support each other's personal growth and development. Encourage learning, self-improvement, and exploration.

3. Adaptability: Be open to change and growth in the relationship. Supporting your partner in her journey of self-discovery and growth can be transformative.

Providing Space

Support also means understanding when to provide space. Sometimes, individuals need time alone to process their thoughts and emotions. Respect her need for solitude when it arises.

Conclusion

Chapter 8 highlights the importance of being a supportive partner in a loving relationship. Emotional support, practical support, encouragement, and allowing space are all vital elements of this role. By being there for your partner in various ways, you strengthen your connection and create a foundation of trust and love. In the chapters ahead, we'll continue to explore strategies for maintaining and nurturing your relationship.

9

Chapter 9: Balancing Independence and Togetherness

A healthy relationship is a delicate balance of maintaining individual independence while fostering togetherness. In this chapter, we will explore the importance of finding this equilibrium and its role in rekindling love.

The Power of Independence

Independence in a relationship means maintaining your sense of self, personal interests, and individual goals. It's vital for your personal growth and well-being. Embracing independence can include:

1. Pursuing Individual Passions: Continue to engage in hobbies, interests, and activities that are meaningful to you.

2. Self-Care: Prioritize self-care for your physical and mental well-being. This not only benefits you but also enhances your ability to contribute to the relationship.

3. Setting Personal Goals: Maintain your personal ambitions and aspirations, and work toward your own goals.

Nurturing Togetherness

While independence is crucial, so is nurturing togetherness. A healthy balance involves spending quality time together, fostering shared experiences, and maintaining a strong emotional connection. This can include:

1. Quality Time: Dedicate time to activities you both enjoy, like date nights, travel, or just enjoying each other's company.

2. Shared Goals: Identify shared goals and aspirations that you both want to work toward together.

3. Emotional Connection: Continue to communicate openly and honestly, fostering a deep emotional bond.

Finding the Balance

Balancing independence and togetherness can be challenging but rewarding. To achieve this balance, consider these strategies:

1. Communication: Talk openly about your need for personal space and shared time. Encourage your partner to do the same.

2. Respect: Respect each other's boundaries and needs for independence without judgment.

3. Compromise: Be willing to make compromises that allow both partners to meet their individual and shared goals.

4. Reconnecting: Regularly check in with each other to ensure that the

balance remains healthy and fulfilling for both of you.

The Benefits of Balance

Finding the right balance between independence and togetherness leads to a more resilient and loving relationship. It allows both partners to grow individually and as a couple, and it reduces the risk of codependency or feelings of being stifled.

Conclusion

Chapter 9 highlights the importance of striking a balance between personal independence and togetherness in a relationship. By nurturing your individuality and maintaining a strong emotional connection, you create a dynamic, fulfilling partnership. In the upcoming chapters, we will continue to explore strategies for sustaining and growing your connection while finding this delicate equilibrium.

10

Chapter 10: Celebrating Milestones and Memories

A thriving relationship is built upon shared experiences and the celebration of significant milestones. In this chapter, we will explore the importance of creating and cherishing memories that strengthen your bond.

The Significance of Milestones

Milestones are markers of your journey together. These could include anniversaries, personal achievements, or even everyday victories. They serve as reminders of your shared history and provide opportunities for connection. Key aspects of celebrating milestones include:

1. Anniversaries: Acknowledge and celebrate the anniversaries of significant events in your relationship, like the day you first met or your wedding anniversary.

2. Personal Milestones: Recognize and celebrate personal achievements, such as career successes or personal growth, with your partner.

3. Family Milestones: Share in the joy of family milestones, like birthdays, graduations, or the arrival of children.

Creating Meaningful Memories

Memories are the building blocks of your relationship's history. They create a shared narrative and a sense of belonging. Here are ways to create and cherish meaningful memories:

1. Travel Together: Explore new places and experience adventures together. Travel often provides rich memories that you can cherish.

2. Traditions: Develop unique traditions that are meaningful to your relationship, whether it's a weekly date night or a special holiday tradition.

3. Photography: Capture moments through photographs. Looking back at pictures can evoke powerful emotions and bring back cherished memories.

Rituals of Celebration

The act of celebration itself is a vital component of rekindling love. It's about making your partner feel special and valued. Consider these rituals of celebration:

1. Gift-Giving: Thoughtful gifts, whether big or small, demonstrate your appreciation and love.

2. Surprise Celebrations: Plan surprise celebrations for your partner. These spontaneous acts of love can be unforgettable.

3. Verbal Expressions: Don't hesitate to express your feelings in words. Offer heartfelt compliments, affectionate declarations, and expressions of love.

Revisiting Memories

Revisiting your shared memories is a way to strengthen your bond. It could involve looking through old photos, watching home videos, or reminiscing about your journey together. Such reflection deepens your connection and appreciation for one another.

Conclusion

Chapter 10 emphasizes the importance of celebrating milestones and cherishing memories in a relationship. These moments help you build a rich history together, create shared narratives, and reinforce the significance of your partnership. By celebrating milestones and revisiting cherished memories, you infuse your relationship with love, gratitude, and a sense of connection. In the upcoming chapters, we will continue to explore strategies for sustaining and growing your bond through meaningful experiences.

11

Chapter 11: Sustaining Love and Growth

Love is not static; it's a dynamic force that requires continual nurturing and growth. In this chapter, we explore the strategies and practices that help you sustain and strengthen the love in your relationship.

The Dynamics of Love

Love, much like any living entity, requires care and attention to thrive. The dynamics of sustaining love and growth in a relationship encompass the following aspects:

1. Continuous Learning: Be open to learning about your partner, her evolving needs, and the ever-changing dynamics of your relationship.

2. Adaptability: Embrace change and be adaptable. This involves adjusting to new phases in life, shifting priorities, and changing circumstances.

3. Investment of Time: Dedicate time to your relationship. This means making your partner a priority in your life and showing her that she's loved and cherished.

Personal Growth

Sustaining love involves personal growth for both partners. As individuals, you should aim for self-improvement and self-awareness. Here's how personal growth contributes to sustaining love:

1. Self-Improvement: Continuously strive to become a better version of yourself. This benefits not only you but your relationship as well.

2. Self-Awareness: Be aware of your strengths and weaknesses, your triggers, and your needs. This self-awareness can lead to healthier interactions and communication.

3. Balance: Strive for balance in all aspects of your life, including work, personal pursuits, and your relationship. A well-rounded life enhances your capacity to love and be loved.

Shared Growth

Sustaining love also involves growing together as a couple. This shared growth is facilitated by:

1. Communication: Maintain open and honest communication about your shared goals, aspirations, and the direction you want your relationship to take.

2. Mutual Support: Be each other's biggest cheerleaders. Support each other's dreams and aspirations.

3. Adventures Together: Continue to explore life as a team, embarking on new adventures and experiences together.

Celebrating Your Journey

Part of sustaining love is celebrating the journey you've been on. This includes:

1. Gratitude: Express gratitude for the love you share and the experiences you've had together.

2. Anniversary Celebrations: Celebrate your relationship milestones and remember the special moments that have brought you closer.

3. Recollection: Revisit your cherished memories and acknowledge how far you've come as a couple.

Conclusion

Chapter 11 underscores the importance of actively sustaining love and growth in your relationship. It involves personal and shared growth, adaptability, and celebrating your journey together. By nurturing your love and continually investing in your connection, you can look forward to a future filled with enduring love, joy, and fulfillment. In the final chapter, we will wrap up the guide to rekindling love and building a lasting, loving future.

12

Chapter 12: Building a Lasting, Loving Future

As we approach the end of this guide, we shift our focus to building a future that's filled with lasting love, happiness, and the promise of continued growth in your relationship.

The Journey Continues

By this point in your journey, you've explored various aspects of nurturing and rekindling love in your relationship. Building a lasting, loving future involves:

1. Reflection: Take time to reflect on how far you've come in the process of rekindling love. Recognize the efforts and growth you've both experienced.

2. Shared Vision: Work together to create a shared vision for your future. Discuss your long-term goals, dreams, and what you want to achieve together.

3. Commitment: Reiterate your commitment to one another. Ensure that you both remain dedicated to the relationship and to the process of loving

and growing together.

Setting Relationship Goals

Setting relationship goals is a powerful way to guide your future as a couple. These goals can include:

1. Communication: Continuously improve your communication skills to ensure you remain open and honest with each other.

2. Quality Time: Dedicate time to fostering a deeper connection through meaningful shared experiences.

3. Growth: Commit to personal and shared growth. Embrace change, adapt to new circumstances, and work on becoming the best versions of yourselves.

The Role of Gratitude

Gratitude plays a pivotal role in building a lasting, loving future. Expressing appreciation for your partner and the love you share is a constant reminder of the beauty in your relationship.

Seeking Professional Help

If you encounter significant challenges or obstacles along your journey, don't hesitate to seek professional help. A therapist or counselor can provide guidance and support in times of difficulty.

A Continual Process

Remember that building a lasting, loving future is a continual process. Love is not a destination but a journey. It requires ongoing care, effort, and dedication.

Conclusion

Chapter 12 serves as a culmination of the guide, emphasizing the importance of building a lasting, loving future. As you continue on your journey together, reflect on the progress you've made, set relationship goals, and stay committed to nurturing your love. Embrace the power of gratitude, and never forget that love is a dynamic force that can grow and flourish with time and effort. I wish you all the best in your ongoing journey of love and happiness.

* 9 7 8 2 1 6 4 3 2 2 9 8 3 *